SO YOU THINK YOU SUCK AT LANGUAGES?

Three astonishing secrets from a school dropout that makes learning a new language so simple it puts college language professors to shame.

Zack van Niekerk

So You Think You Suck at Languages?
Copyright © 2021 by Zack van Niekerk
All rights reserved.

CONTENTS

Dedicated to the beautiful people that I've been blessed to meet with, speak with and share ideas with.

THE BEGINNING

I remember the heat against my skin, the sun glancing off the water's ripples as my toes drooped lazily, hairs standing on end, into the cool blueness. A distinct *cock-a-doodle-doo* from behind the large wooden shed nearby. Ripe figs hanging temptingly over my head.

Sounds beautifully poetic, right? Well, it was.

I'd only been in Spain a few days at this point, fresh-eyed and bushy-tailed at the age of eighteen. Elizabeth, the brown-eyed girl I'd fallen for, sat next to me. The noise of the pool became a welcome distraction from my stuttering, which was partly caused by my lack of knowledge of the language and partly due to nerves.

A love affair had begun.

And no—in case you're wondering—not with the Spanish girl beside me. Don't get me wrong, I liked her, but it was nothing more than an eighteen-year-old's infatuation. My love affair was with something more precious than any crush, and it would empower me to live a very unique life.

I fell in love with *learning*.

I found myself in a very small village of around 18,000 people in the south of Spain, around sixty kilometres from the historic city of Granada. I had managed to secure myself a job at a market stall, selling leather belts and slippers. Glamourous, I know! My Spanish skills were rubbish and I had very limited resources at my disposal. No internet, no course books, no teachers, only a dictionary. Despite this, after only six months, I was fluent in Spanish, cracking jokes and holding in-depth conversations.

You're probably thinking, "Sure, but being surrounded by Spanish people 24/7 must have made learning the language easy." Well, no, not really.

There were many expats living in Spain, and in my first year, I encountered many of them. Some had lived there for well over a decade. Despite being inundated with the Spanish language, people, and culture on a permanent basis, many—in fact the vast majority—still couldn't speak a lick of the language.

Besides the local presence of a lot of English speakers, another issue I had was the accent. The area around Guadix had a very unique one. To put it in perspective, imagine you're an English learner and you suddenly find yourself in a very remote area of Scotland, where the accent and colloquial phrases have no resemblance to anything you've heard and studied. Everything, absolutely everything, sounds alien to your ear.

Well, that's what it was like facing the accent of Guadix.

On top of this, learning in itself was something I knew little about. I mean, that's what teachers are for, right? They guide you through the process, give you what you need at each junction, and correct you when you make a mistake. They give you structure, tell you what to learn, and give you a timetable so that you stick with it. But I had no teacher, no coursebook, no app, no internet, an accent I couldn't hear past, and little idea of how to move forward.

Yet, these apparent problems became a blessing in disguise. I went on to master not only Spanish but also Chinese at a fluent level and to teach hundreds to do the same.

I went through a natural process of elimination. I would try a technique, and if it worked, I continued to use it. I was obsessed with the idea of learning something quickly, and as these methods and learning ideologies became more concrete, I began sharing them with others.

The results were spectacular.

I saw my students progress faster than they—or I, for that matter—ever thought possible. The methods I had organically developed worked. My students spanned all age ranges and educational backgrounds. My youngest student was eight and the oldest was eighty-six. One thing was clear, these methods worked.

Now, here's the curveball: I'm no genius polyglot and I never went to university. In fact, I took two languages at school, German and French. I was kicked out of my German class at twelve and ended up leaving school at sixteen with a C in French. So, how on earth did I come to write a book on learning languages and, more importantly, why should you dedicate your precious time to reading it?

If my school result is anything to go by, it may seem like I'm terrible at learning languages. For a period of time I believed that. In fact, if I'm honest, to this day I don't consider myself a talented language learner, despite speaking Spanish and Chinese fluently.

One thing I do understand is how to learn efficiently when everything is against you. I spent over a decade trying countless methodologies and reading every article and book I could find on the topic of learning. The combination of learning and trying over again was the catalyst for the content of this book. It's been a process of trial and error and the result is this book, which will allow you to bypass everything that I've been through.

The truth is, most people don't have the time or resources to go through the process I went through of "figuring things out," and this is why I wanted to share the content of this book with the world. I want you to become fluent in a second language, and I know that you *can* achieve it with the right help.

Of course, I don't know your personal situation, but I'm sure that, like most people, you have a busy schedule, hopes, desires, and aspirations, and you deserve to achieve great things. If you want to learn a language, then my belief is that you should have access to the knowledge that will get you there. I want to make learning a new language achievable for everyone.

Life is beautiful when you continue to learn new things. A spirit of continual self-education makes you a more interesting person, multiplies your friendships, sets you up to earn more money, and ensures you an extraordinary life. And this is what's so powerful about learning and why I want to share this book with you.

Bridging that gap between saying "I want to learn a second language" and "I'm fluent in a second language" can be tricky. Taking the first step can be the easy part: Buying a book, downloading an app, joining a course, hiring a tutor, or watching some YouTube videos are some common strategies. The most difficult part, however, is seeing it through to the point where you're fluent—in other words, never giving up.

The fact that you're not fluent in a second language right now is not your fault, and whether you know it or not, you already possess the skills, intelligence, and resources to do it. You may not believe me at this point, but it's true. It's just a question of harnessing and directing the assets, or *superpowers*, you already have and knowing how to use them to reach your goal.

That is the purpose of this book.

I will teach you *how* to learn organically, in a way that's in harmony with the resources you already possess. You will learn how to do this with the Three Pillars. These Three Pillars form the foundation that will allow you to reach fluency in any language you choose to learn.

Now, there are some things you won't find in this book.

You won't find long lists of vocabulary to memorise. You won't find lessons on grammar and the syntax of language. There are literally thousands of books and courses that cover these points in great detail. Instead, I want to give you practical tools to actually learn successfully with little to no resources, no matter your age, perceived intelligence, educational background, or whether you think you have a good memory or not.

This book is designed to give you the tools you need to start and finish learning a language. Once you grasp the concept and principles that sit behind how to learn, you will be able to handle any of the minutiae, like grammar and syntax, easily. It's just like the age-old adage, "Give a man a fish." If I just gave you grammar rules, this would be giving you a fish. Instead I want to teach you *how* to fish, *how* to learn, so that you can learn any aspect of any language easily.

The book will focus on two basic time frames when it comes to learning. First, what you should study in your first few days of learning. Then, how to make sure that you never stop learning until you're fluent.

I will show you how to ensure that you're always excited to study and learn—in other words, that you never lose steam. Many struggle with the consistency and commitment needed to keep the book they just bought from collecting dust on the shelf and actually read it all the way through. Learning a language is a process that takes time, there's no getting away from it. However, when you understand how to do it properly, the process becomes a lot easier and faster.

To kick things off, I have one task for you. Write down the language that you want to be fluent in:

Cool, now let's get stuck in!

THE THREE PILLARS:
AN INTRODUCTION

I want to kick off this section by letting you in on a surprisingly little-known fact.

We're lucky, to a large extent, with the amount of resources we have at our disposal. Most people in modern society have the opportunity to attend higher education of some sort, not to mention the sheer volume of information we can access at our fingertips instantly via the internet.

Okay, this is no magical revelation. You know this already. Thanks to Google, everyone is an expert.

Despite having all of this information ready at the tap of a finger, the secret to mastering a language does not lie in buying the best coursebook or app, going to the best university, living in the country where they speak the language, or possessing talent or huge amounts of time or money.

None of this is the secret.

Imagine you want to start going to the gym. You want to get in shape and make a habit of working out. You identify the gym you want to go to and buy all the necessary gear you need—the clothes, the shoes, the bags, everything.

You have everything you need. However, you still don't go.

Having these resources at your disposal does not mean that you will go to the gym every week, month after month.

I'd like you to answer the following questions with a simple yes or no.

1. Do you have access to the internet?
2. Do you have access to a smartphone?
3. Did you finish school?
4. Did you study languages at school?
5. Do you have $10 spare to spend on a book?
6. Have you learned a foreign language fluently after the age of eighteen?

If you answered yes to questions one to five and no to the final one, then hopefully you will understand the point I'm trying to make. Having all of these popular resources *available* does not mean that you will be successful in learning the language.

Let's address the common tendency to think that the secret is moving to the country where they speak the language in question.

I remember being confused when I first arrived in Spain at the age of eighteen and began meeting expats who had lived there for years.

They were immersed in the language every day, yet they could hardly speak it. I've seen this phenomenon in every country I've been to, from Germany to China to Portugal to France. As I write this paragraph, I'm sitting in a coffee shop in Prague, where I've been living for the last three months. I've met countless people who moved here years ago from America, the UK, Italy, and other countries. Most speak barely any Czech. If you are an expat living in a foreign country, you will know exactly what I'm talking about.

The main reason for this comes down to our natural inclination to find the path of least resistance. When you move to a foreign country, it can be very easy to only hang out with people who speak your native language. The familiarity is comforting. So, your new community becomes one where you only speak your native language. This path is an easy one to travel down, and unless you make a concerted effort to divert from it, that's where you stay.

The secret doesn't lie in a course, a book, a teacher, or even living in the country where they speak the language. These are tools that you can use to improve your level of the language, but having *access* to these things doesn't mean you will bridge the gap between wishing to learn a language and actually doing it. So, if the secret doesn't lie in these things, where does it lie?

We are accustomed to solving every problem externally. If we're hungry, we eat food; cold, we wear warmer clothes; lonely, we watch TV or hang out with friends; sick, we get medicine from a doctor. Our lifestyles are all about getting the solutions for our needs externally.

The internal power that we possess, however, is not only remarkable but is also often dumbed down by the sheer amount that we consume. Understanding the immense power and ability that you already have inside you and learning how to harness it is vital to your success.

It comes down to understanding two things. First, the barriers between you and fluency, and second, the mechanics of actually learning efficiently. Think about it for a moment. You know that you want to learn a second language. You also know that you have almost unlimited resources at your fingertips, and yet, the truth is, you still haven't reached your goal yet (*yet* being the big word here!).

Before the age of airplanes, travelling across the Atlantic was not only expensive but a long and difficult journey. With modern technology, that trip is now quick and relatively inexpensive. What happened? The barriers were removed. Money was a barrier, and now it's comparatively much cheaper. Safety was a barrier, and now it's a lot safer.

Let's take a moment to look at some of the most common barriers many face when they try to learn a new language. I'm going to go over these pretty quickly, as a lot of these barriers will be automatically broken down once you complete this book. Having said this, it's important to have a clear vision of what they are.

1. **Cost** – "I don't have enough money to pay for education"
   I get it. Life is expensive, and spending money on something like learning can be way down on our list of expenditures.

The good news is, you don't need to spend a lot of money. In fact, I learnt Spanish fluently for a total cost of around $15—that's it.

2. **Intelligence and Education** – "I'm not clever enough" or "I'm not good at languages"
   Okay, it's true that there are some very talented individuals out there that seem to have a God-given gift for learning languages. You're not one of them? Well, neither am I. I tell you what, though: You can speak your native tongue fluently, right? As can billions of people on the planet. You have the *ability* and *skill* to do it because you've actually done it already. It's just a question of tapping into that skill and understanding how to harness the power you *already* have. You will learn how to do this.

3. **Difficulty** – "It's just too hard"
   It's true that learning a language is not the easiest thing you will do in your life, but it's a lot easier than you think. You just need to know how to do it! Once you're equipped with the knowledge and skills to achieve this goal, it will be a lot easier than you imagined.

4. **Tried and Failed** – "I've tried to learn before and made no progress"
   Yep, this happens a lot. It's not because you're *bad* at learning, it's just that nobody showed you how to learn in the right way, in a way more in harmony with who *you are*.

5. **Lack of Desire/Incentive** – "I'd love to learn a new language, I've bought all the books and courses, but I never actually get down and study"

   Yes, yes, yes. I've heard this barrier said a gazillion times, and the truth is, it can affect us all—not only when it comes to learning, but in every aspect of our life. You will soon have the tools so that you will never again say, "I just don't feel like it".

6. **Time** – "I don't have the time to study"

   Life is busy. However, when you learn based on the Three Pillars, you will understand how to do two things. First, you will learn to maximise your time so that you study efficiently and with intention. Second, you will understand how to immerse your life in the language easily, without sacrificing your daily routine and obligations.

If you feel like any of these barriers apply to you, don't worry; you're in good hands. The purpose of this book is to not only help you see that these barriers aren't actually a big deal, but also to put you on a path where they don't influence your chances of success.

A big factor behind these barriers is our relationship with learning itself. This relationship is shaped in many ways depending on our home life and education. Because of past experiences, many people develop an unhealthy relationship with learning, and this can sometimes lead them to feel like they aren't capable of learning a new language from scratch.

Learning is much more than a classroom, a teacher, and a book. It consumes our life in so many complex ways. Understanding our inherent and natural ability to learn is the secret to success.

Now, it's time to get stuck into the meat of the book: the Three Pillars!

THE FIRST PILLAR:
THE RIGHT STUFF

I want to take you to the Philippines for a moment, where a local pearl diver is about to resume the hunt. He has everything ready; he has greased himself up to conserve his body heat and he is holding on to a heavy rock that will pull him to an approximate depth of twelve metres.

It's going to be a hazardous dive. He'll be battling unknown sea creatures, the cold temperature, and the lack of oxygen with no breathing apparatus or modern gadgets to assist him.

He begins his dive, trying to keep as calm as possible while the bright sunshine above him diminishes. He doesn't look up, instead concentrating on the task ahead of him. He sinks to the seabed and, releasing the large rock in his arms, begins his search.

It's been a meagre month for him as a diver, and he hasn't seen much success. His livelihood depends on his dives into the ocean, finding and selling pearls. The pressure is always on. He has to find something good, and soon.

Suddenly he sees something—a large oyster jammed in between two very large rocks. Inside of it, he sees as he swims closer, is a large pearl staring back at him in all of its perfect beauty.

As he tries to free the oyster, he soon realises that it's wedged a lot more firmly than he thought. He can feel the growing pressure in his chest as carbon dioxide begins building up in his blood. In his profession, timing is vital, and now he has to make a decision. Should he keep trying to free the oyster, or should he dive again to retrieve it? He knows after many years of diving that there is a distinct possibility he won't have enough oxygen left in his lungs to free the oyster and make it back to the water's surface.

His decision is based on the difference between two things: what is important and what is vital.

When you begin learning a language, you can face a similar dilemma (though the stakes are probably lower). You're confronted with thousands of courses and books, and the language itself will often have tens of thousands of words to learn. Where do you begin? Do you focus on grammar? Reading? Writing? Memorising words? Memorising entire sentences?

Your goal is to communicate as much information as possible, as quickly as possible. In order to do this, you need to be ruthless with what you study—especially at the beginning. This is the subject of the First Pillar of Learning: *content*. The substance of the information that you dedicate your time to.

Much like the diver, you must choose to begin with what is vital; to approach studying any other way can mean death to your success. Your early stages of learning are the most critical, beginning with your very first hour of study. If you get that right, you will set a solid foundation for your progression to fluency. If you get your first week of study right, then the second week is easier to get right, and then the third week, and so on.

We have a problem, though. We've never been officially shown how to do this. How do you decide what you should spend your time studying?

The Simple Spectrum

I want you to imagine a spectrum that goes from one extreme to the other. On the left side we have simple content and on the far right we have complicated content. As time progresses, the content increases in complexity.

Traditional academia has the challenge of teaching thousands of students at exactly the same time. When a syllabus is created for a class, this general spectrum is used to define what you study on a chronological schedule from the first day of class to the last. First, you learn what is simple, and the complexity of the content you study is gradually increased; it's the same for all students.

Although it may seem like a logical way to define and organise content, it has a huge problem for the individual in question. Take a look beneath the surface and you'll see a very important factor is missing.

Practicality.

Let's take the subject of mathematics as an example. Students begin with basic arithmetic. As the years progress, they move on to slightly more complicated topics such as algebra and trigonometry. This process continues right up until they graduate, and when asked the question, "Do you understand basic math?" they can answer, "Yes, I do".

So, what's the issue with this? School did the job, right? Well, yes and no.

According to the Survey of Consumer Finances conducted by the Federal Reserve Bank in the USA every three years, the average debt of under thirty-fives is $67,400. That debt continues until old age, with the average debt of over seventy-fives being $34,500.

Now, imagine you were taught the *practical* side of mathematics at school—that is, money management. Imagine investment strategies were included in the syllabus for all children. Imagine there were specific modules on debt, its dangers, and how to use it for your benefit. Imagine what would happen if every teenager came out of school understanding how interest rates worked and the basics concepts behind profit and loss.

This is mathematics with a practical, everyday application that you never touch on at school. Focusing on practical content has a lot of advantages for the individual studying. Now, I'm not proposing that we change it per se—well, perhaps I am, but I'll leave that discussion for another time. Rather, I want to introduce another way of choosing the content you study, content that is more in harmony with *you* and *your* needs. I want to show you how to make what you study more individualised.

The main idea of the First Pillar is that both spectrums—that of traditional academia, and the *practical* spectrum—work in harmony with each other from the very beginning.

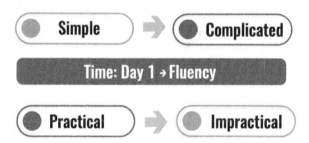

At the very beginning of your learning process you should be focusing on the content which is practical as well as simple. What we're talking about here is you choosing your *own* content. Content that you will actually use, that is applicable and specific to you.

Let's dive in to see how it's done.

The Skeleton Method

Your brain is an amazing machine capable of so much, but it's also brutally efficient. Your brain automatically relegates impractical, useless information to last place when it comes to memorising new things. With that in mind, vital content is the most practical content for your individual circumstances, needs, and goals.

This is where the Skeleton Method comes into play. The Skeleton Method is how we all naturally and organically learn from infancy, but fine-tuned into a framework that you can apply when you first begin learning something new. This strong foundation, the skeleton, is composed of a group of around five hundred useful and practical words. Its purpose is to get you communicating as efficiently and as quickly as possible.

Imagine you're stranded in the jungle. You know night is about to fall and a storm is about to rage. What's your priority? Obviously, it's to attain some cover and safety so that you're protected when darkness arrives and the storm hits.

This is your goal when you first begin learning a language. As quickly as possible, you must curate an arsenal of words that you can use in the most common situations you'll find yourself in. These words need to be ready to go, ready to be used as soon as possible in your learning journey.

This is how the best language learners on the planet do it. That's right—children.

Children don't start with complicated, grammatically correct sentences when they are just learning to speak. They begin by crying, babbling, and laughing, a simple but effective form of communication, and their tactics and skills gradually increase in complexity as they get older. What they communicate is not only simple, but it's also directly correlated to what they *need* to communicate in a given moment. They organically communicate what is vital for them. If a baby is hungry, tired, sad, or happy, they communicate these needs and emotions in the simplest and fastest way possible. This lays a solid foundation for them to function and survive, and as time progresses, the complexity of their language increases (as do their needs and emotions).

This is the focus of the Skeleton Method. As time progresses, you will add to your skeleton with the meat that brings you to a nuanced and fluent level.

Here is an overview of the Skeleton Method and the different steps that lead you to fluency.

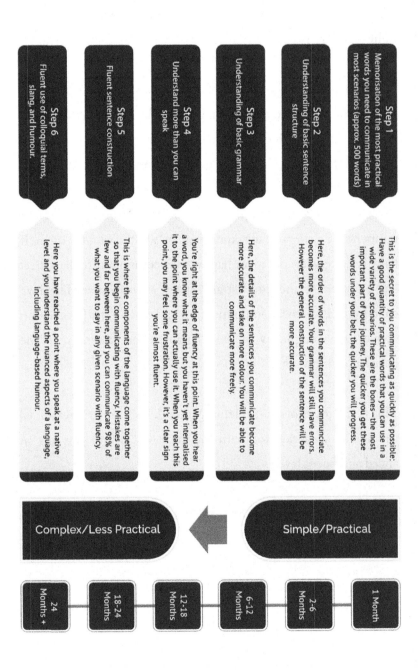

Step 1
Memorisation of the most practical words you need to communicate in most scenarios (approx. 500 words)

This is the secret to you communicating as quickly as possible: Have a good quantity of practical words that you can use in a wide variety of scenarios. These are the bones – the most important part of your journey. The quicker you get these words under your belt, the quicker you will progress.

Step 2
Understanding of basic sentence structure

Here, the order of words in the sentences you communicate becomes more accurate. Your grammar will still have errors. However the general construction of the sentence will be more accurate.

Step 3
Understanding of basic grammar

Here, the details of the sentences you communicate become more accurate and take on more colour. You will be able to communicate more freely.

Step 4
Understand more than you can speak

You're right at the edge of fluency at this point. When you hear a word, you know what it means but you haven't yet internalised it to the point where you can actually use it. When you reach this point, you may feel some frustration. However, it's a clear sign you're almost fluent.

Step 5
Fluent sentence construction

This is where the components of the language come together so that you begin communicating with fluency. Mistakes are few and far between here, and you can communicate 98% of what you want to say in any given scenario with fluency.

Step 6
Fluent use of colloquial terms, slang, and humour.

Here you have reached a point where you speak at a native level and you understand the nuanced aspects of a language, including language-based humour.

Complex/Less Practical

Simple/Practical

1 Month

2-6 Months

6-12 Months

12-18 Months

18-24 Months

24 Months +

At this point, your goal is to communicate as quickly as possible, and the first step in the Skeleton Method has this goal at heart. Many focus on the latter steps of the Skeleton Method too quickly and instead of helping them communicate it actually slows them down. Imagine a painter trying to paint the details of an iris in a portrait before he's actually prepped the canvas and sketched out what he's going to paint. Right now, your number one focus will be to build a group of practical words that you can use in any scenario. Although you will not be speaking fluently like a native, that's okay, as having these words under your belt will get you talking quickly!

There are three simple steps that you need to follow to get this going, and this is what we're going to focus on now. Remember, you're only going to be focusing on increasing the number of *words* you can use in different scenarios. You're not going to worry about putting together full sentences.

An overview of the process is shown in the following diagram.

01	Define 5 specific physical places where you will speak thelanguage
02	Extract 5-10 of the most practical words you would need in those places
03	Translate those words to your target language

Let's look at each step in more detail.

Step 1

Learning a language is all about communicating, and the vast majority of communication happens in real time, face to face. The first step is to define *where* you will use the language you're learning. These are specific places and scenarios where you're physically faced with the need to communicate in the new language. This is where your attention needs to be focused when you first begin studying, that face-to-face time in real-life scenarios. Choose the most practical and common scenarios you find yourself in, and then learn content associated with those.

The scenarios will be broken down into two sections: organic and artificial.

The organic scenarios you choose will be where you have no choice but to speak the language. This could be an upcoming holiday, business trip, or date, to name a few.

Artificial ones will be where you have no pending or organic need to use the language you want to learn. If you're sitting at home on a sofa in the north of Scotland wanting to learn Arabic, you may not have any organic need for the language in question.

Many begin learning a language with the desire to become fluent. They dream of how awesome it would be to actually speak it. This is great, but when you begin, you must be specific. Where will you speak it? What words will you need to communicate in these scenarios? This is how to kick-start your learning journey.

Here's an example of how you might go about defining those scenarios.

Organic Scenario Example: A Business Trip

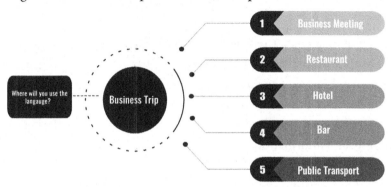

Artificial Scenario Example: Useful Places to Prepare For

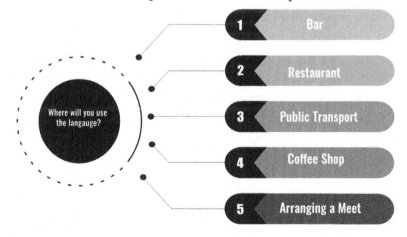

Whether the scenarios are organic or artificial, you must identify specific places. Once that is done, move on to the next step.

Step 2

Now that you have the five scenarios identified, the next step is to extract the words you are going to need in those scenarios. Don't worry about grammar here, just focus on downright useful words that, above all, convey the main ideas you want to get across.

Imagine you're in a restaurant and you want to say the sentence: "This is a fantastic dish. I absolutely love it!" You want to say it like a native. You want to sound perfect in your new language. And so, you dedicate time to memorising that sentence word for word. But, remember that your brain is ruthless when it comes to filtering out non-useful information.

Also keep in mind that you have the basic capacity of learning five words per day. Let's say that you dedicate your time to learning all the words necessary to put together this sentence—a total of nine words, or perhaps slightly more or less depending on the language you're studying.

When you realise how much time you need to invest in order to memorise a full sentence and then consider what you get out of it, you know it's not worth it.

This is why you need to simplify things.

When you simplify what you want to say in order to get your idea across, it speeds up your ability to communicate. For example, we could simplify the sentence "This is a fantastic dish, I absolutely love it!" to "Good food!"

Studying the two words *good* and *food* is much more practical than dedicating an hour to memorising the entirety of the original sentence. Of course, saying "Good food!" is not as eloquent as saying, "This is a fantastic dish, I absolutely love it!" But don't worry about that for now.

Remember, your focus when you first begin learning a new language is to share the most important ideas as quickly as possible, not evoke Shakespeare!

You need to have razor-sharp focus when you first begin. Concentrate on learning what is absolutely vital for you to communicate in a specific, real-life moment.

With that in mind, you must now extract between five and ten words for each scenario you've identified. Take, for example, the scenario of a bar.

These are generic words that, when said in the right scenario, will ensure that the person you're addressing will understand what you need. Repeat this process for all five scenarios.

Imagine trying to paint a house before the foundations are built. Obviously, that would be impossible. Before a house gets painted, a good foundation needs to be laid and the walls need to be constructed and prepared. Increasing the amount of practical vocabulary you have to use *is* the foundation of that house. Once the foundation has been laid, you can then paint your language skills with more complex vocabulary and grammar.

This is exactly what happened when my brother joined me in China.

I had been living in China for one year already when my brother moved out from the UK to join me. He spoke no Chinese at all when he arrived, so watching what he learnt over the first few months was fascinating to observe. Chinese is a complicated language in many ways, with a vocabulary of tens of thousands of words. It is completely different to anything he knew in his native language of English.

I helped him apply the Skeleton Method in an organic way, focusing on the most practical words he needed in the scenarios he was finding himself in. Very soon—within days—he was able to manoeuvre around the city by himself. He learnt the words necessary to survive. It started off with basic words to use at the shops and then gradually progressed to words he needed at a restaurant, in a taxi, and then in basic conversations.

Now, he is fluent and still lives in China.

The way I learnt Chinese is also a good example of this. I approached it in a very different way than everyone else I knew who was learning it at the time. Most of them, in fact all, put a lot of their time into reading and writing Chinese. Me? Zero time. I didn't care about reading or writing at the beginning. I only focused on communicating in the scenarios I would find myself in, and I did that as quickly as possible. Now, the interesting thing here is that I began learning Chinese in Spain. So, like you, perhaps, I was faced with the reality of not having a community around me that could speak the language.

Because of this, I had to artificially create the need for myself. It wasn't going to magically find me. So, I patronised Chinese restaurants and shops and made them my playground for growth in the language, gaining as much vocabulary as possible to use in those two specific scenarios.

My progress was three times as fast as anyone else around me, even those that were attending the best language college in Alicante, the town where I lived in Spain. As time progressed, so did my grammar. Thus, my metaphorical skeleton was plumped with the meat of hundreds of words and grammatical constructs that I had not only memorised but used in real situations.

Growth is your goal. And choosing practical content, specifically practical vocabulary, is key to incredibly fast progress. I'll sum it up here:

Creating or defining the need and then extracting the content you study from that need is the big secret to becoming fluent very quickly.

The diver at the beginning of this chapter had to make the distinction between what was important and what was vital, and you need to do the same with content when you first begin. Study practical content based on your needs.

So now you have your starting point set, a group of twenty-five to fifty of the most practical words you can think of that you will need for your chosen "common scenarios". You've defined those scenarios and then extracted the most practical words in those scenarios.

Step 3
The next step is to translate them into the language you want to learn. The simplest and quickest way to do this is to copy and paste them into Google Translate, which is a very powerful tool for learning languages. Once they are translated, do two things: First, copy and paste them into an electronic document that you can access later, and second, spend fifteen minutes writing the words down in the notebook that you have set aside specifically for learning your new language. The process of writing it down—notice you're not trying to memorise them yet, just writing them down—will help reinforce the words in your mind.

This process can be repeated until you have a solid group of five hundred of the most practical words that you need and will actually use.

Now that you've done this, you have a group of words that will form the basis of beginning to study your new language. Now that you have the list, you need to actually get them into your brain, your memory, so that you never forget them. This is what we will look at in the Second Pillar.

Summary

When you first begin learning, focus your attention on the right areas of content, in harmony with yourself and your needs. Just like the pearl diver, your window of opportunity to get the momentum and speed necessary to carry you through to fluency is relatively small. This is why, in the early stages especially, you must have laser focus directed towards defining the most practical content.

- Throw all your effort into learning practical content when you first begin.
- Define five of the most common scenarios that you will find yourself in, either organically or artificially.
- Extract the most powerful and practical words in your mother tongue that will convey as much information necessary in your chosen scenarios, in the shortest amount of time.
- Translate these words into the language you want to learn and write them down.

THE SECOND PILLAR:
THE RIGHT WAY

If you wanted to cross the English Channel and travel from the south of England to France, a distance of 21 miles at its narrowest and 150 miles at its widest, how would you do it?

You could swim it. Many have achieved this, with the record being held by Alison Streeter for having swum across it an insane forty-three times. With the right training and preparation, it's possible. But is swimming really the best method of transportation?

Well, if your goal is just to get from England to France, you could take the Eurotunnel, a tunnel that runs for twenty-three miles underneath the sea and allows for the quick travel time of two hours between London and Paris. You could also fly or take the ferry.

There are different ways of reaching a destination, and some are faster and more efficient than others. You'll want to choose your method of transportation based on what you want out of the journey.

Learning a language is exactly the same.

The method you choose to get you to fluency will affect how quickly you achieve it, how pleasurable the process is, and your chances of success.

How you approach learning will have a massive impact on how successful you will be, as effort does not equal output. You've probably heard the saying, "Work smart, not hard". Well, it applies to language learning, and this brings us to the Second Pillar of Learning: *method*.

In the last chapter, we spoke about what you learn, and the focus was on practical content you will actually need to use in real scenarios. Now, you need to go ahead and learn these words.

This is the part that scares off a lot of people. You may think that you don't have a good memory, you're not talented at languages, or that it's just too much work to remember new words. If you feel this way, I understand. However, I'm going to help you with this.

Step back in time with me to my high school, Bedford Modern, and walk with me to my biology class taught by the—dare I say it—iconic Mr. Maisey. I think everyone had a Mr. Maisey at school. His curly grey hair and his growly voice, in combination with his foul temper, has stuck in my memory ever since. He would stand at the front of the classroom and etch word after word on the large blackboard with his back to us. He would just write and write and write. And his students? Well, we had the joy of copying down what he was writing.

Riveting.

Now, let's say that what he was writing was amazing, useful, practical, and interesting content. Maybe it was. But I can't remember any of it, and why? Because the method he was using to teach us was… what's the word I'm looking for?

Terrible.

Let's shift to my French class with Mrs. Mitchel for a moment. There was an inevitable moment at the end of each class where she would say, "Okay, now memorise these twenty words by tomorrow". Without any more prompting or guidance, that was it. *Learn the words.* How? We would have to figure that out ourselves. Repeat the words again and again? Write them on Post-it Notes and stick them around the house? Those were pretty much all the "methods" I had at my disposal.

This is the problem.

Throughout my entire fifteen-plus years in traditional academia, I never learnt *how* to learn. I don't want to knock my teachers, or any teacher for that matter, as it's not their fault. No one taught them how to learn, so how could they be expected to help me do it?

The content—which was based on the simple-to-complicated spectrum we went over in the previous chapter—would be chosen and organised in the form of a syllabus and handed out to the students. Some teachers were good and tried using methods that they had invented or stumbled across, but that was just luck of the draw.

Read this book, memorise these words, study this article. That's all I heard, without ever being shown *how* to read or *how* to study or *how* to memorise. All in one go? Should I make notes? Should I read it out loud? It was all a guessing game, and unfortunately for many people today, it still is, through no fault of their own.

So, if you think that you're bad at learning new things, there is more to it than meets the eye.

Learning how to learn is one of the most important and useful skills that we're never officially taught. Content and method are two separate things, and content is only useful to you if it's assimilated into your mind via a method that makes it useable. Otherwise it's about as valuable as a tent in a tornado.

Let's focus in on what this means for you.

Everyone has the capacity to remember. It's an integral part of who we are as humans, and without that ability, we'd end up dead very quickly. We'd forget that boiling water is dangerous and that knives can cut. Everyone remembers. I want you to think of your favourite memory for a moment. It could be from when you were a kid or when you went on a fun holiday. My brain goes back to when I was twelve, and my mother and I spent the entire day walking through the English countryside. I can still see so many details clearly in my mind's eye. I remember the taste of the cake that morning at the small coffee shop, how the kernels of wheat felt in my fingers as we walked through the fields. I remember the smell of the bacon and egg baguette that we got at lunch time as if it were yesterday.

The brain's creation of a memory is dependent on a complex system of many things, but we can summarise it quite simply. It comes down to how our senses interact with new information. Our senses allow us to create the memory of that amazing cake, or how the sea looked that day, or the smile of our friend. These memories are imprinted on our mind *because* of our senses.

Your senses are the door to memory.

Now, most of the time, this is a process that happens naturally. Your senses interact with the outside world, and if it makes an impression, well hey, presto—you have a memory. If the new information you encounter doesn't interact properly or to the right degree with your senses, your brain judges it as unimportant and relegates it to the bottom of the memory pile.

The secret to this Pillar is understanding how you can *manipulate* your senses to interact with new, practical content you wish to remember, so that your brain creates new powerful memories, locked and loaded into your brain for you to access whenever you need them.

Everyone has memories, and everyone has the power to remember anything. They just need to be shown how.

In my online courses, I go over dozens of powerful techniques you can use to do this, but to get you started in this journey, I'm going to discuss the powerful principles that govern all the methods that I teach. From this, you can not only begin learning new content effectively today, but also begin defining a way of learning that works for you.

Principle 1: Quantity and Quality

Many people fall into the trap of trying to learn too much in a very short space of time. The result is that you actually learn less, considerably less in fact. The principle here is swapping things around 180 degrees.

Spend more time studying less.

Let me repeat that.

Spend more time studying less.

My recommendation is to learn a maximum of five words per day. If you dedicate twenty to thirty minutes per day on only five words, you will give your brain a chance to assimilate and remember that information. Keep in mind the content needs to be quality (the First Pillar). When those five words are well-chosen, practical ones, you're on target for real success. Remember that you can't fool your brain; if the content isn't genuinely practical, your brain will struggle to remember it.

Giving new content the best possible chance of being transferred into your long-term memory is a key principle of learning something well. And this comes down to studying a small amount of words consistently.

Your learning behaviour has been trained by your time in academia, where you're normally given a lot of largely impractical material over a short period of time. Give your brain space to breathe by focusing on less and learning it better. So, how do you do this?

Principle 2: Your Senses

Your brain interacts with the world around you fundamentally through your senses: sight, hearing, smell, taste, and touch. Your beautiful, extraordinary brain is a tool, and it relies on your senses to access, assimilate, and understand new information. Use it right, and it will help you; use it wrong, and it will do its own thing— which probably won't be in harmony with your goal of reaching fluency in a new language.

The secret to becoming a speed-learner of a language is to employ as many of your senses as possible to learn *one* new piece of information. The more of your senses you employ, the easier it will be to remember that new information.

An important aspect to this principle is making sure that the way your senses interact with the new information is intense. Think of a few strong memories—any will do. Those memories weren't created just by your senses being involved. You use your senses 24/7, right? Specifically, it was *how much* stimulus the new information provided to your senses. For example, imagine an amazing concert. The atmosphere, the lights, the sound of the crowd, the smell of the sweaty cologne of people dancing around you, and then the well-rehearsed performance. It made a huge impact on your senses, and that's how a vivid, lasting memory was formed.

Generally, when we refer to making an impact on our senses, we look at a stimulus that produces an extreme reaction. This reaction could be humour, sadness, excitement, frustration, or any other of our countless emotions. The more extreme the effect on your senses that the new information has, the more impact and permanence it will enjoy.

Let's look at some practical examples of this.

Sight

This is probably the most obvious one. If you want to learn something new, you need to get your eyes involved. Write down new words. Use different colours, make it beautiful. Sketch a picture of what the new words mean (you might draw a cartoon and make it funny). Read the subtitles as you watch a film. The main idea: Employ your eyes as much as possible in interesting and fun ways.

Hearing

Get your ears involved in hearing the new information. Sounds simple, but you can get very creative with this. Record yourself and listen back to it. Listen to the words being spoken by a native. Record them saying the word on your phone and listen back to it. Listen to a friend saying the words. Listen to music, the radio, or a film.

Taste and Smell

Taste and smell may not be as obvious as the latter two senses. However, they can also be extremely powerful when reinforcing new information into your memory. You might try connecting a word to a dish which is famous in the country where they speak the language you're learning. For example, why not cook one such dish while learning the words relevant to dining in a restaurant? The taste and smell of that evening will give your brain a massive boost when it comes down to remembering those new words. Or why not have a cocktail night when you make drinks from the country where they speak the language in question and then learn the words for a bar or café that you may have compiled in the First Pillar?

The magic of employing your taste and smell when you learn is that you can make the learning experience more fun and exciting. Trust me, if you host a Spanish night where you get a bunch of friends together and eat paella, and then try and learn five new words in Spanish, you'll never forget those words!

There is no law against having fun as you learn, and I cannot stress this enough. You need to be creative with how you allow your senses to interact with new information.

Touch and Movement

Touch and movement will often be involved whenever you employ the other senses. One really powerful method for employing touch is creating a specific gesture for every new word you learn. You can almost create your own sign language in order to prop up the new words you're learning. Create a dance routine where each new word is linked up to each dance move. Writing is the most obvious manifestation of touch when we're talking about studying.

You can also walk and run as you learn. The increase of blood flow to your brain as you do this will also give your brain an extra boost!

Are you beginning to get the idea here? Being creative with how you take in new information makes it memorable!

When you think of a memory, any memory, you notice there is hardly ever just one sense involved. You remember the sounds, the smells, the look of everything that was involved in the creation of that memory. Think of a baby, a perfect example of an organic learner. As a baby grows up, it is surrounded by new sounds, new smells, new textures, new tastes, and new objects and people to look at. All of this information feeds into the brain to reinforce new information. Why must this babyhood habit fizzle as we age? Why do we limit our senses' involvement when we learn something new as adults?

At this point, you may be thinking that all this sounds like a lot of work. And when you first start, it may indeed feel like it. But when you start seeing results, you will soon forget the "work" you put into it. We've been trained to associate learning with a classroom and a teacher, but creating a powerful learning environment around yourself, where you employ your senses and immerse yourself completely in the new information you're studying, will be worth going that extra mile.

When you learn by yourself, it shouldn't be boring. You can engage all your senses as much as you like when you learn something new. This will make the process fun and, more importantly, help you to never forget what you learn. Don't just "study" something and then move on; immerse yourself in it. If you're learning Spanish, bring Spain to your home, and completely immerse yourself in the culture even though you aren't actually there.

Principle 3: Use It or Lose It

In the First Pillar, we focused on studying content that is practical. Something only becomes practical once you use it. You don't over-buy food with the intention to throw it away, do you?

There is something magical that happens in your brain when you put what you're learning into use. You're learning a language so that you can communicate with it, so, get communicating—no matter how basic your language skills are. If you've learnt one word, use it.

There are a few ways that you can make sure that you actually put what you're learning into use.

1. Have a regular practice session with your study buddy.
2. Travel to the country and use the language as much as you can.
3. Hire a native speaker to have coffee with you and practice one on one.
4. Go to language exchange meet-ups. If there isn't one organised in your town, organise one yourself. Even if just one person shows up, it will be worth it.
5. Practice with yourself if there is no one else to practice with. This is something I had to resort to often. I'd go for walks and practice the language to myself over and over again.

The main idea here is to USE IT!

When you start applying these three principles to learn new information, the results will be impressive! The great thing is that they're not only extremely powerful, but also practically free. Before we move on to the final Pillar, spend a few minutes and brainstorm how you will implement these principles to learn the words you've identified in the First Pillar.

We have a problem, though. We've defined all of this great content, and we know the methods we should be applying to remember it, but we don't do it. For some reason, we don't take the action necessary to make it a reality. Why and how can we overcome this?

That question brings us to the final Pillar.

Summary

- The goal is to remember, so spend more time studying less content.
- Involve all of your senses when learning one new piece of information. This is organic learning.
- Immerse yourself completely in what you are learning. If you can't move to the country, bring the country to your home.
- Use it or lose it! Use what you're learning as quickly as possible and continue to do so from your very first day of studying.

THE THIRD PILLAR:
THE RIGHT MOJO

Throughout my life and career, I've heard many say regretfully, "I wish I could speak a second language". This remark plagued me for a long time. The people who said it had money, resources, intelligence, and every possible asset they might think they need to succeed. But more often than not, that passing wish stayed as such, with no progress, year after year.

What was missing? Why do some people go for it and others don't?

A car without petrol is nothing more than a fancy tent, and a human without proper fuel is just as stationary. We need petrol inside of us driving us toward the goals we set for ourselves. You might have the best content in the world and knowledge of the best methods in the world, but it's not enough. These two things by themselves will not guarantee fluency or mastery over what you're learning.

Although the first two Pillars are vital to success, there is one more. The final and most important Pillar of Learning is *desire*.

Desire is your petrol, the fuel inside of you that makes you do incredible things despite immense barriers. I'm not speaking about a whim or a passing wish like, "I'd love to do that someday". I'm talking about an internal passion, a yearning to achieve something specific no matter what, and you actually do it. Desire is what compels you to dedicate precious time to studying and ensures that you stick at it until you master it, no matter what the barriers are.

Anyone can start, but only those with real and true desire will keep going until they reach mastery.

Imagine you want to make a fire, but all the firewood surrounding you is wet from an earlier rainstorm. To add insult to injury, it starts pouring down again. It is possible to make a fire that will stand on its own, despite the wet and cold; however, it needs be started quickly, and then get big and strong quickly, in order for the flame to survive.

This is the desire that I'm speaking about.

No matter what barriers life throws at you, no matter how much it "rains" on you, your internal desire to achieve your goals will be so strong that you still achieve them.

You've no doubt had this experience yourself at different points in your life. Perhaps it was starting a business, getting healthy, or some other kind of goal. You did it with determination, no matter what obstacles rose to meet you, and you achieved your goal.

That is the main purpose of this Pillar—to set you up for complete success in your learning journey, no matter the challenges. You understand the importance of practical content and the importance of the right methods; now we need to ensure that you continue learning until you're fluent. No stopping. Continuous dedication to the goal no matter what, right up until the moment where you can proudly say, "I'm fluent".

So, here's the big question. How can you create and stoke the "desire fire" inside you if you don't have it? Is this even possible?

The good news is, it is possible, and that's what I'm going to show you now. No matter what your educational background is, whether you think you're clever or stupid, or whether you're eighteen or eighty, you can learn to curate this desire within you.

So, here's an overview of what we're going to look at.

First, we will look at the fuel that stokes this "desire fire" in you specifically. Sadly, this is something that we were never really shown how to identify in school, despite its importance.

Second, I will introduce you to the Circle of Desire, an endless loop that allows you continually throw wood into your "desire fire". This is a proven method to organically grow and fuel your passion and desire for learning. I stumbled across this concept by accident after analysing what kept me going as I learnt Spanish and Chinese to a fluent level, as well as my other endeavours in the fields of business, health, music, and photography.

Let's get started.

Secret 1: Petrol or Diesel?

If you put petrol into a car that uses diesel, you're going to find yourself facing a hefty bill. The same applies to learning. *You* have a specific fuel that will dramatically stoke your passion for learning. Although all of us are of the same species, we each have our individual hallmark. We each have our own tastes, personalities, hopes, and dreams.

When you were at school or university you were in the same course as hundreds of other students, and as a national collective, thousands (or more) of other students. Each student was studying the same material in much the same way. The same books, the same course, and the same exams. This uniformity does not allow for individuals to discover what really makes them tick. Of course, some students will discover it, but it's often something that happens by chance, as opposed to something that is integrated into the way we're taught.

Let's spend a few moments figuring out what makes you tick.

First, you need to have a good understanding of the building blocks of your personal passions, the tinder that allows your desire to burn bright. For you to understand this, I'd like you to think of THREE activities on THREE separate occasions over the last ten years that you loved so much that you wanted to do them again and again. These activities could be anything from knitting, to sports, to perfecting the technique of frying an egg, to travelling somewhere. Any activity. The only important aspect is that you loved it so much that you wanted to do it again.

Activity 1:
Activity 2:
Activity 3:

Now that you've defined these three activities, I'd like you to think of three to five characteristics for each activity that contributed to your love for it. I call these Longevity Characteristics, or LCs. Was it the people you were with? The adrenaline you felt? The sense of achievement? Was it how relaxing it was? Think about *why* you enjoyed it and what made you want to *continue* doing it and not give up. Remember, this exercise is specific to you and you can choose any activity you want.

You may automatically respond, "Well, it was fun. I enjoyed it. That's why I wanted to do it again". However, I want you to think about *why* you enjoyed it and wanted to do it again.

Allow me to share my top two activities. I learnt Spanish and continued to learn until I was fluent. I love photography, so I continued studying it until I became a professional photographer who gets paid to take pictures. I love playing guitar, so continued studying until I became a proficient guitarist.

	Activity 1: Spanish	Activity 2: Photography	Activity 3: Guitar
Longevity Characteristic 1	I *love* how I connect with new people that I would otherwise never meet.	I *love* how photography is something that I can do with friends and family.	I *love* how it allows me to express my creativity whenever I want.
Longevity Characteristic 2	I *love* having a unique skill that makes my life richer and more interesting.	I *love* how I can get results quickly and see the creative results of my efforts.	I *love* how I can play guitar with friends and enjoy time together.
Longevity Characteristic 3	I *love* how, as I learnt the language, travelling took on a whole new dimension of awesome.	I *love* how learning photography gave me more work opportunities.	I *love* how I can use my guitar skills to earn money.
Longevity Characteristic 4	I *love* tackling the puzzle of a new language and trying to simplify it.	I *love* tackling the puzzle of learning how to take good pictures and trying to simplify my technique.	I *love* how creating music makes me feel happy.
Longevity Characteristic 5	I *love* how learning the language gave me more work opportunities.	I *love* how travelling takes on a whole new dimension when I incorporate photography.	I *love* how playing the guitar makes me a more interesting erson.

Use the boxes below to write down your own personal LCs for your chosen activities. It may take a few minutes to figure out what you *love* about the activities, but it's worth the time.

	Activity 1:	Activity 2:	Activity 3:
Longevity Characteristic 1			
Longevity Characteristic 2			
Longevity Characteristic 3			
Longevity Characteristic 4			
Longevity Characteristic 5			

After that's done, let's take a look at what you've written down. What you will notice about your own personal LCs is that between these three activities there are common threads, or patterns, that emerge. We want to focus on these patterns.

If I look at my LCs for the three activities I chose, I see that the big ones they have in common are travel and social interaction. These are specific to me and my personality. From this pattern, I now know what I need to love about something in order to continue doing it. I know that if I learn something new, the process of learning *must* involve meeting new people and travelling (and increasing my work opportunities, for another shared LC). That is what's important to *me*.

Go over your LCs again and highlight TWO which indicate a pattern between the three activities:

LC 1:
LC 2:

Since these passion-fuelled activities and their LCs are specific to you, there is no right or wrong answer here. Actually, I take that back—there is a right answer, in a way. The right answer would be you being true to yourself and identifying what gets you going. The wrong answer would be regurgitating what you believe other people feel is "right" or "better".

Whatever your reasons are, they're your reasons, and that truth is powerful.

Once you've identified your patterns, you need to incorporate these characteristics into the way you learn. The sooner you do so, the happier you will feel as you learn—and happiness is always the goal! You need to enjoy the process of learning so much that you do not want to stop, and the quickest and simplest way to do this is to introduce your personal LCs into your learning programme.

By way of an example: Let's say I decide to learn French. I know that travel and human interaction is something that makes me enjoy a specific activity. So, the first thing I would do is organise a trip to France with a friend who is also learning the language. I would incorporate my personal LCs into my learning journey. As I live in Europe, this is something I could easily organise. I would then, in conjunction with my study and travel partner, set the specific goal and focus of using the language *as much as possible* during the trip. Scheduling this trip would be the first step I would take in my learning journey. Before I left for France, all of my learning would be focused towards being able to communicate in the scenarios that I would likely find myself in on that trip.

Both travel and the promise of good company tick boxes as very attractive LCs for me, as well as giving me a massive boost to help me learn French. During my day-to-day study at home, I would also make sure that I integrate these two patterns into my weekly programme. For example, I might arrange for a group of people to get together to practice and study French together once per week, and I would make it a social, enjoyable occasion. There would be good food and wine and socialising in conjunction with learning.

Write down three activities that you can plan to help you succeed in learning your new language, making sure they are in harmony with your personal LCs.

Learning Activity 1:
Learning Activity 2:
Learning Activity 3:

Now that this is done, you will automatically start to feel more excited about learning—I guarantee that. Spending five minutes defining what gets you going when it comes to learning is a powerful tool to achieving success.

Let's now look at the second secret within this important Pillar of Learning: the Circle of Desire. This is where everything I've discussed thus far converges.

Secret 2: The Circle of Desire

Where I grew up as a young kid in South Africa, we'd often set up what we call a "foefie slide" (pronounced *foofee*), otherwise known as a zip wire. Here's the thing about a foefie slide: Even if you're scared, you're still going to get to the end of the line because you're strapped in. No matter how scared you feel, no matter how much you scream once you lift off, you'll only stop once you reach the end.

This is the goal of the Circle of Desire (COD) philosophy—creating a perpetual circle that takes you from beginning to learn something to mastering it, no matter what life may throw at you, which can sometimes be a lot.

The COD, once implemented, will enable you to continue learning right up until the point that you become an expert. It's almost like a train that won't stop; it will automatically carry through to the completion of your goal.

The goal of the COD is to get and increase your *desire,* and it has four key components:

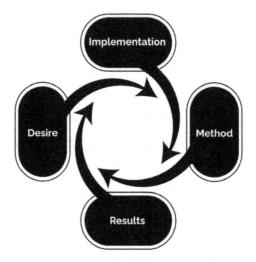

Each of these components feeds into each other and works in unison to boost and maintain your desire. The beautiful thing to this method, though, is that focusing on each individual step actually ends up removing the negative influences that life may throw at you.

As we look through each of these components of the COD philosophy, you will soon see how easy and important it is to have it built into the way you approach learning anything, and how everything we went over in the first secret of this Pillar will be of great use to you too.

Let's begin with the first step in the process.

Implementation Framework

Implementation is a no-excuse step when it comes to the COD. Granted, it can be the most difficult aspect of the roller coaster that is the COD. So, what exactly does "implementation" mean in this context?

Imagine you want to learn a language. You want to be fluent. You go to a book shop and buy a new book, feeling excited. You tell your friends that you've got this amazing book.

Let's fast forward six months. That book has grown a healthy layer of dust as it sits on the bookshelf. You did the first chapter and half of the second, but you stopped there. And so, your plans to learn a new language disappeared. This is where the first component of the circle steps in with full force.

So, you want to learn a second language?

Great. Begin!

Well, we all know it's quite as simple as that.

Tomorrow is a weird thing because it always comes around, right? There will always be another morning and another evening—until there isn't and it's too late. Sad, but true.

Here are six things that can help you actually get started right now:

1. *Have a clear understanding of the benefits of speaking a second language.* It will improve your friendships, work opportunities, and the way you live in general. Write them down and remind yourself of them every single day.

2. *Don't fall into the trap of overbuying books and courses.* Having too many choices can actually paralyse us when we want to learn something. I've seen people with literally dozens of books on a skill they want to learn, and yet they haven't actually read a single one. It's better to study one mediocre book cover-to-cover than own fifty of the "best" learning guides and not read one.

3. *Keep yourself accountable by telling friends and family.* Telling others about what your plans are helps solidify it in your mind and will encourage you to get rid of your fear of judgement and failure.

4. *Set time aside in your diary to study.* I recommend an absolute minimum of one hour per day, however this can be spread out into increments such as three twenty-minute sessions over the course of a day. Whatever you decide, remember it cannot only be adjusted, but it must be planned out in advance. Try to sync it with another habit in order to make it easier to complete; before breakfast, after dinner, or during your daily commute to work are a few examples.

5. *Acquire the materials necessary to actually begin studying.* These are a good dictionary, a large and a small notebook, and a space that you will use to study—whether in your

house or a coffee shop. Wherever it is, it's your space, a place that you feel comfortable and good about studying in. Make sure that you connect this place with studying.

6. *Communicate your study times with those you live with.* Let them know that you've set aside this time every day to reaching fluency in your new language, and make sure that the time you are going to study (even if it's just five minutes) is set in stone.

Once you do these things, beginning will be so much easier. The clearer you plan out *how* you're going to study the language, the easier it will be to actually begin. Now that you've got all the pieces ready to begin studying, you're ready for the next stage of the COD.

Method

In the chapters on the first two Pillars, you learnt the key techniques that you need to apply in order to learn quickly and efficiently. This comes down to defining the most practical content you can, then giving your brain the best chance of remembering this new information by exercising all of your senses to learn the new information, and then putting it into practice as quickly and as often as possible.

A vital component to this method is attributing your Longevity Characteristics as much as possible to everything you study. By now, you have a good understanding of what makes you enjoy something, so when you actively try to implement those things into your study habits, the whole process will automatically be more enjoyable.

Now that you've begun to put everything into practice, you're ready for the next stage of the COD.

Results

One goal you should set is to regularly achieve short-term wins. Short-term wins are the building blocks of long-term wins, so focus all your energy on these. It will not only make you feel great, but it will ensure that your progress is measured and clear cut. Rome wasn't built in a day. Remember, you have the power to define your own short-term wins.

There are three aspects to defining short-term wins.

1. *Your short-term win needs to have a finale.* That finale could be a family member testing you on words that you've learnt or ordering food in a restaurant only using the language you're studying. If the finale is clear, then the win will make you feel positive about your progress.
2. *Reward yourself once you achieve the win.* Put some money in a holiday fund, cook yourself a nice meal, give yourself a gold star, or share your progress with your friends and family.
3. *Track your progress.* Write down what your quick win will be, and once it's completed tick it off. This will keep you motivated as you continue to achieve these quick wins.
4. *Write down what your short-term win will be.* There is something magical about writing down a goal. It clarifies and cements it in your mind and on paper.
5. *Communicate what your short-term wins will be to someone else.* Telling someone about your goal does two things: It once again solidifies the goal in your mind and increases your accountability for actually reaching it.

Here are some examples of short-term wins that you could set yourself as goals:

- Order food in a restaurant.
- Buy tickets on public transport.
- Start a simple conversation with someone.
- Speak about your hobbies, dreams, or plans in your new language.
- Speak about your work—what you do specifically and why you like it—in your new language.
- Master five new words in a day.
- Spend one entire day just speaking in your new language (no matter how basic).
- Learn how to swear in the new language.
- Translate a poem.
- Write a poem in the new language (no matter how good or bad it is).
- Learn a song in the new language (no matter how good or bad it sounds).

There are endless examples of short-term goals you can set yourself that will be fun and interesting and help you enjoy the process of learning.

You need to make proactive decisions to follow the goals you set yourself—and make sure you write them down!

You see, nothing comes by itself.

If you want to climb a mountain, you need to make sure that you've got the correct equipment, the route planned, and a method of transportation to the mountain. Learning a language can seem like climbing Mount Everest at times. If you do want to climb Everest, you don't start with Everest. You start with smaller climbs, smaller mountains; and each time you climb a slightly larger mountain—or, in other words, achieve a slightly larger goal—you achieve a positive result that brings you closer to scaling the peak of Mount Everest.

Now you may ask, what happens if you fail at the quick win that you are trying to achieve?

It's a valid point, and I understand that fear of failure is a powerful barrier to many. It's important you remember that failure is a positive part of the process and it will happen. Everyone—and I mean *everyone*—who is successful has failed many times over. That is the very characteristic that defines their success. You have no idea how many mistakes I've made learning languages. I've never considered myself good at languages, but I am good at working hard to get quick wins consistently, no matter how many times I fail.

When you fail, it's an indicator that you are making progress. If you aren't failing, you aren't progressing—please remember this! Failure provides you with a fantastic opportunity to highlight the areas that you need to work on, which is always positive.

When I first began learning Spanish, I tried to put what I was learning into practice and achieve these quick wins that we're speaking about here. However, despite my best efforts, I'd often mispronounce or misspeak, and a native speaker would not understand me.

A huge failure, right? Well, not quite.

It enabled me to eventually find out from the native speaker how to say the word correctly. They would often model how a native pronounces the word and tell me the ways in which it can be used. That failure allowed me to grow in what I was learning in really positive ways. If I wasn't searching for results and welcoming failure, this would never have happened.

When you push yourself to achieve positive results from the very beginning, you will feel a spike in your progress, as well as—more importantly—the final part of the COD.

Desire

This brings us to the last section of the COD. Everything we've spoken about up until this point has the specific goal of increasing your desire to study and learn. Desire is your tinder, your fuel, that makes sure you never stop. Your cup of desire needs to be filled to the top, brimming over the edge as the main catalyst that drives your study.

It's a unique part of the COD philosophy, as there are no actions involved. Desire is a by-product of doing all the other steps right.

If you follow the first step, implementation, and then focus on the right content and methods, and then strive to achieve lots of quick wins, your cup of desire will always be full. It's exciting to think that by following this formula, you can reach a place where you're so excited to learn that, no matter the barriers you face, you will continue studying day after day until you reach fluency.

This is the power of desire. When your cup is full, you're motivated to restart the circle again and again, renewing your desire with each cycle.

Interestingly, you must still work to keep your cup full. When a person is sick and starts taking a prescribed medication, they may be tempted to stop taking the medication as soon as the medication starts to work. In some cases, this may be fine, but in others, feeling better is a by-product of the ongoing functioning of the medication, and in order to maintain that feeling, they need to continue taking it.

When we feel good, it can be easy to slack off and stop implementing the COD, but remember that in order to maintain that feeling, you need to continue to follow each step.

The lesson here is simple: results, results, results.

Summary

- Understand your personal Longevity Characteristics, what makes you tick. Once you understand what makes you enjoy dedicating time to a specific activity, implement that factor into your study routine as soon and as often as possible.
- COD Step 1: Implementation. Prepare to begin by putting everything in place in your life, so that beginning to study is as simple as possible.

- COD Step 2: Method. Apply the first two pillars as quickly as possible when you begin studying. This means studying practical and simple content by applying memory techniques to memorise the words swiftly.

- COD Step 3: Results. Focus on getting results quickly. Make sure the results are specific to *you* and *your* needs.

- COD Step 4: Desire. Enjoy feeling the joy of progress as your cup of desire fills up. Use the desire to propel you back into the first step of the COD.

THE FINAL STEP

So, how you feeling? I hope you're excited! I want to congratulate you on reaching this final section. It demonstrates that you genuinely want to learn a new language and you're determined to make a success of it. Now, you may also feel a little overwhelmed, and that's okay.

Keep this in mind: You've learnt the basic principles and skills that will allow you to be successful as a language learner, and that is an *incredible* beginning. Now, it's important that these don't just stay theoretical. Start using them in your life today.

At this point, let's recap what you've learnt over the last few chapters to really solidify everything in your mind.

First Pillar: Content. Your goal here is to identify a group of practical words that you will actually need and use. Begin by defining where you will be, then use those scenarios to identify the specific words you need to learn. Focusing on learning useful vocabulary at the beginning of your process is the secret here.

Second Pillar: Method. This is where you begin memorising the words from the First Pillar. Use as many of your senses at once to learn new information. Make it interesting and exciting, and don't be afraid to go all out with your imagination!

Third Pillar: Desire. You need to make sure that you always have the desire to study. First, put everything in place so that beginning is easy-peasy. Then, apply the first two Pillars as efficiently as possible. Then, focus on getting results, short-term wins, that are specific to you. When you achieve a quick win, celebrate it. Then repeat the cycle.

Now that you understand these three concepts, you are in a position to be truly successful at learning a new language. Despite this, there is one more important secret sauce to your success.

You have everything to gain in the future by learning a new language. You'll make your life even more amazing. You will get more friends, your self-confidence will increase, you will become more intelligent as you exercise your brain muscle, and you will become a much happier person. These perks comprise the utter joy that learning a new language brings you—if you choose to accept the challenge.

You have the power, knowledge, and resources at your disposal to make this journey a real success, and it's something that you *will* achieve as long as you take to heart and apply the Three Pillars you've learnt in this book.

I want to give you one final goal: *Never stop trying.*

Set yourself this goal right now because the truth is, despite every technique you've learnt and every principle you've seen, consistency beats any technique hands down. Even if you don't apply the methods you've learnt about in this book, if you're consistent in your desire to reach fluency and you make learning a part of your daily life, you will reach your goal. When you combine consistency with powerful methods, then that journey becomes even easier and faster.

Share your knowledge with your friends and family to help them become better learners too. Not only will you be showing them how to improve their lives, but the very process of sharing what you learn will further reinforce it in your memory.

So, go do it! And as a parting gift, I'm going to share with you my biggest lesson of all. Out of everything we've learnt, this is what I want you to remember:

MAKE IT FUN.

Made in United States
North Haven, CT
16 September 2022

24204740R00046